THE THORN*i* ___

A selection from the poems of
Fran Landesman

sun tavern fields
1992

Cover design by Danusia Schejbal.

ISBN 0-9517012-1-5
A catalogue record for this book is available from the British Library.
Copyright 1992 by Fran Landesman.
Published by sun tavern fields, PO Box 982, London E1 9EQ.
Typeset by Counter Productions, London.
Printed by Antony Rowe Ltd, Wiltshire, Great Britain.

Contents

Not Your Night

When you looked in the mirror you were lookin' good
And you started the evening in a dandy mood
Now you're feeling neglected and misunderstood
It's not your night

As you sipped your Martini all your moves were great
But your gambits made no impression on your date
Now you toy with the pasta bleeding on your plate
It's not your night

Why don't you try to relax and say goodbye to that frown
It's just another night out. Another night on the town

You were dead on arrival at the restaurant
Which is done up like Ali Baba's favourite haunt
Now a nice graceful exit line is all you want
It's not your night

There's a singer who's murdering your favourite song
As you sit there and wonder how it all went wrong
You're an island of Chekhov in a Dallas throng
It's not your night

Seems like the harder you try the more the scene gets you down
It's just another night out. Another night on the town

So you're under the weather and you're overdressed
Paranoid, suicidal and a bit depressed
You're just one more disaster in the dying West
Old friend, it's not your night
But try to keep it light
It's just another night
On the town

Jumble Sale

I found him at a jumble sale
A slightly damaged adult male
His hair was thin, his skin was pale
His eyes were grey, his health was frail
He'd done a little time in jail
But still he was an English male

I found a velvet hat with veil
A woollen vest, a plastic pail
A yellow T-shirt lettered YALE
A painting of a stranded whale
And quite complete in all detail
A slightly damaged adult male

At last my strength began to fail
The air was growing rather stale
And so I hit the homeward trail
To have my tea and tell my tale
Of battle at the jumble sale
And wash and press my adult male

I Quite Like Men

I quite like men. They're rather sweet
I like to give them things to eat
They have nice hands and charming necks
And some of them are good at sex

My sympathies are feminist
But I am glad that men exist
Although they can be perfect swine
They're nice with candlelight and wine

They warm me up when I feel cold
And some of them have hearts of gold
They irritate me now and then
But on the whole
I quite like men

Selling Our Secrets

We're all selling our secrets
Trying to gain some visibility
Grabbing a handle on celebrity
We're telling our tales

We're all selling our stories
Making the most out of a love affair
Laying the seamy inner landscape bare
We're making some sales

What the great man said. How he was in bed
With a picture spread
So we turn a trick - we're just doing *shtik*
Till they make the flick

We're all spelling it right out
Stripping the attics of our private lives
Stories of buggery and murdered wives
The sex, the star trips, the scenes
Telling our secrets
Selling our dreams

Crown Of Thorns (for Jeff)

With the crown of thorns I wear
Why do I need a prick like you?
If you choose to bugger off
It isn't going to spoil the view

I've been put down by the best
And crucified by experts, dear
And I really do not need
A friend like you to bend my ear

You claim that generosity
Is something that I lack
May I suggest you've had from me
Much more than you gave back

So don't think I'll mope and mourn
Because you tell me that we're through
With the crown of thorns I wear
I sure don't need a prick like you

Portrait Of Nobody

On your desk there's a picture of nobody
And nobody calls you on the phone
You make plans to have dinner with nobody
You wake up and find that you're alone

Once your hours were crowded with somebodies
They played Space Invaders with your heart
Now you reach out for no one and nobody
And nothing is tearing you apart

No matter how you tried
No one was satisfied
They threatened suicide
To stay beside you
Now there is no one home
Inside your pleasure dome
And you no longer roam with love to guide you

You are matched up and married to nobody
You've driven the lovers from your life
There is only the ghost of a melody
The memory of someone else's wife

You return the affections of nobody
And nobody's stories make you yawn
You explain your departures to nobody
And nobody will notice when you're gone

Little Old Love-Maker You

There's a lady in London who loves you
There's a Lord and a sailor or two
And some talented girls who are tearing their curls
Over little old love-maker you

I am sure you must charm the gorilla
And the seals when you visit the zoo
The smooth and the rough simply can't get enough
Of little old love-maker you

And even I have fallen, who once stayed so aloof
The thought of you affects me like rolling off a roof

You have lovers all over Manhattan
They don't do you much good it is true
You seduce everyone but it isn't much fun
For little old love-maker you

There's a lady in London who loves you
And a cat and a budgie or two
And even a goat who is slitting his throat
Over little old love-maker you

You Make Me So Nervous

You make me so nervous
You make me so tense
I snap and I stammer
It doesn't make sense

You make me so nervous
I talk much too fast
And when we're both happy
I'm scared it won't last

The pleasure you give me at moments
Is more than my pen can express
But why do you give me the feeling
That I'm such a terrible mess

When you're in a bad mood
You make me so sad
I simply can't bear it
You're driving me mad

But all of my worries
Dissolve when we touch
You make me so nervous
I love you so much

Shoes

I don't know why I let you stay
But I just can't refuse
We have a smoke and right away
You're taking off your shoes

You haven't got a word to say
No gossip, jokes or news
I mention it's a rainy day
You're taking off your shoes

This isn't what you'd call romance
We tell no tender lies
I never even get a chance
To look into your eyes

The love we make is cold as death
It's not what I would choose
Before I even catch my breath
You're putting on your shoes

I wish that you would stay and eat
Or have a little talk
But you just knock me off my feet
And then you take a walk

Our crazy loving goes so fast
You've got no time to lose
I try to make the moment last
You're putting on your shoes

Morning Song

He comes to see her in the morning
When the sun shines on her bed
The sheets are scented by her body
And the dreams still in her head

At first he crawls in bed beside her
And they lie there still as spoons
And then his fingers touch her body
Till he finds familiar tunes

Sometimes they spend the day together
And sometimes it's love and run
He comes with other little blessings
Like the milk, the mail, the sun

He sees her early in the morning
With the sleep still in her eyes
He puts a pillow underneath her
And they find the way to paradise

Come Here, Go Away

Come here, go away
That is what I hear you say
Hold me tight but let me stray
I don't fancy it today

Come here, go away
Learn what signals to obey
Now I want you. Now I don't
Now I'll kiss you. Now I won't

Please tell me what you really think
No, never mind I want a drink
You're looking wonderful tonight
What makes you think you're always right

Love me now and then
There's no way of knowing when
It will be your lucky day
We'll call you when it's O.K.

Love dies, love is made
Feeling makes us feel afraid
Please don't touch me
Now you may
Come here
Go away

Just Along For The Ride

Used to be I was just along for the ride
In the snapshots a smiling face at your side
Mr Big Shot's a wee bit bored little bride
Just along for the ride

Home from work you expected me on my knees
Drinking scotch you were distant and hard to please
Wife and mother, I always felt ill at ease
I kept losing my keys

Now here I am at that terrible age
When women surrender to boredom and rage
Suddenly feeling this isn't the end
And you, my old jailer, are more like a friend

Used to be I would dream about suicide
Now I write about feelings I used to hide
If I blow it at least they'll know that I tried
And I'm not anybody
Just along for the ride

Mother

M is for my masochistic urges
O is for the ordeals I endure
T is for the tear-drop that emerges
H is for my line of horse manure
E is for my poor deflated ego
R is for the rotten life I've led

Put them altogether they spell
      MOTHER
The woman who fucked up my head

Find Me in Bed

You can find me in bed if you want me
If you want me that's where I will be
With the ghosts that continue to haunt me
And a nice cup of peppermint tea

You can find me in bed if you want me
In my bed where I choose to abide
I'll accept any favours you grant me
If you want me lie down by my side

Slide down the path of dreams with me
Into the sea of night
Its velvet tides will hide us from
The torment of the light

I'll be here lying back on the pillows
Staring out at the black marble sky
Where the moon hides her face in the willows
And the wind sings of danger on high

You must know I'll be happy to have you
For the poems that are locked in your head
If you're looking for someone to save you
And you want me you'll find me in bed

With All My Hats

I love you with all my heart
And with all my hats
I love you with both my hands
And my Siamese cats
I love you with all my books
And my two big toes
I love you with both my eyes
And my shiny nose

I hope you find some room for these
Small tokens of my affection
I've also got a hive of bees
And a beautiful sky collection

I love you with all my heart
And my records too
I want you with all my words
And the colour blue
Please take all the songs I make
Or they'll fall apart
I love you with all my hats
And with all my heart

And the Birds Refuse to Shine

Then kiss me goodnight this morning
If your madness matches mine
I'll stay till the sun stops singing
And the birds refuse to shine

I'm yours till the early warning
And we're gonna do just fine
Till banners have lost their spangles
And the birds refuse to shine

Till the grass runs out
And the mountains move
If I'm by your side
You can call it love
But if you should say
That my poems were lies
Then you've never seen
Through my X-ray eyes

I'm yours till the sun stops singing
Till the darkness wins the war
When Frankenstein loves his monster
It won't matter any more

I'm yours till the floor stops swinging
If your madness matches mine
I'll stay till the sun stops singing
And the birds refuse to shine

The Argument

All we did was argue
All we did was yell
Any day at our house
Was any day in hell
When they died I never cried
I couldn't shed a tear
But in my head I try to win
The case they'll never hear

They said that I was impudent
And lazy and incompetent
So now I'll never rest content
'Cause I can't win the argument

They made me feel like nothing
They made me feel so small
The funny love they gave me
Was worse than none at all
Now I'm grown and on my own
I can't forget their words
They twitter in my tired mind
Like flocks of angry birds

Though I present my evidence
Their ghosts aren't easy to convince
They'll never let me rest content
'Cause I can't win the argument

In Another Country

I was living easy
On the edge of crime
In another country
In another time

It was just a party
Where we laid it down
In another language
In another town

There was crazy music
Till the crack of dawn
He was sweet and evil
How we carried on!

I was still a stranger
On a foreign shore
Every day was different
Every night was more

Why should I be sorry
For that long lost year
In another country
Far away from here?

Do you smell his shadow
On your clean white bed?
But that's ancient history
And the man is dead

That was in another country
And the man is dead

Crazy Sundays

The crazy Sundays come and go
The globe is spinning fast
We meet again to lose ourselves
With darkness falling fast

We've been to parties up and down
From Hampstead to the Grove
Been crucified by butterflies
And tantalised by love

The ashtrays fill, the glasses spill
The clown and killer flirt
They scratch the itching sore of lust
And wish that it would hurt

It's fine to see professionals
Play hide and seek with pain
But in the end it's you and me
And back to bed again

The pictures on the ceiling dance
The music echoes on
You never let me fall asleep
Till all the stars are gone

I am not in my perfect mind
I have been much abused
I will not swear these are my hands
My senses are confused

So be not grieved by words of mine
For sure I am your friend
And I'd be more than sad to see
Our crazy Sundays end

The Eros Hotel

Let's go up to the Eros Hotel
And write some love songs on the sheets
We'll climb the dusty carpet stairs
That smell of hurried love affairs
Old victories and defeats

There's a bar in the Eros Hotel
It's like a party all the time
That's where you meet the unicorn
The young man with the golden horn
They all know how to rhyme

I've never been alone with you
I don't know how good we would be
And if we should collaborate
Would the music of you fit the lyric of me?

Let's go up to the Eros Hotel
And write some love songs on the sheets
The sheets are worn as soft as sin
From all the loves that might have been
The sweet sonatas of the skin at dawn
At the Eros Hotel

How Come?

How come she ever lost
All the hope she never had?
What was it that she wanted from the start?
How come she ever cried
For the dreams she never tried
And couldn't learn the secrets of the heart?

She longs to go back
To where she's never been
The way that she plays
She's never gonna win

How come she can't stay home
And can never be alone
With nightmares that she's never gonna face
How come she's killing time
With no reason and no rhyme
It's sad the way her beauty goes to waste

She longs to go back
To where she's never been
The way that she plays
She's never gonna win
She's fragile as an angel made of snow
How comes she hugs the thorns and can't let go?
And how come
I love her so?

The Heart of Darkness

The darkness which clings
To everyone's heart
Is the door to the mystery
The gateway of dreams
Two twilight figures
The shadow and the echo
Step into our visions
And twist all our schemes

And we've done it all
And we are possessed
By the snakes that breed
In the raven's nest

And the fairy tales
On a dusty shelf
Are the only clues
To the buried self

Haunted by dreams from our misty beginnings
We tangle our lovings and heap up our hates
Walking through minefields we dare not discover
That spooks in the closet are sealing our fate

And the shadow's song
And the echo's eyes
Weave a spider's web
Of seductive lies

There's a sweet perfume
On their poisoned breath
As they drag the Prince
Down the road to death

And the only clues to the buried self
Are the fairy tales on a dusty shelf

Lost Lovers

Have you seen them in a restaurant
Photogenic couple turning grey
Each inside a separate sealed-off world
Sitting there without a word to say?

Wonder if they do it any more
Could it go that way with you and me?
Isn't there a way to beat that rap?
Isn't there a way to get home free?

Have you seen them in their house of glass
Alcoholic glow-worms in their eyes?
Anger gives them just the edge they need
Cutting their old sweetheart down to size

If I stay with you another year
Will we start to fall into that trap?
Dining out without a game to play
Isn't there a way to beat that rap?

Have you seen them in their Gucci shoes
Tapping out a message of despair
Run-arounds out shopping for a dream?
Could we ever grow so sad and square?

Oh my love, I'll miss you if you go
I can feel the ice begin to crack
Once I had a friend who made me laugh
Isn't there a way to get him back?

Unlit Room

I'm in an unlit room
In an unmade bed
Feelin' like I'm almost drowned
I'm just an unknown bird
In an unkind town
Wishin' I was outward bound
I'm the unsung hero
Of an unwritten romance
That never did get off the ground
I'm in an unlit room
In an unreal world
Feelin' like I'm almost drowned
Oh baby
Take me to the lost and found

Wasted

Wasted are these days that I don't spend with you
Wasted are my empty nights
Wasted are these mornings and this postcard view
Wasted all the spring delights

Tasted once the happiness your love could bring
Tasted what your lips could do
Now the falling blossoms and the fireflies
Are wasted like my love for you

Wasted are these scenes that I don't share with you
Maytime melting into June
Pasted on the ceiling of this velvet night
Sequins, stars and silver moon

Wasted are the letters that I never send
Wasted are the poems I pen
Wasted my creations and my crazy dreams
Till I'm in your arms again

Christmas Blues

The Christmas truce is over
It's really such a bore
We've eaten all the turkey
So now it's back to war
I don't know why you tarry
It all seems such a waste
And after Christmas pudding
You leave a bitter taste

I've got the Christmas blues, the Christmas blues
The kind you can't drown in an ocean of booze

We gave each other presents
We really tried to please
We filled the children's stockings
Hung tinsel on the trees
But after Christmas dinner
The brandy and the Queen
There's nothing to console us
Except the TV screen

I've got the Christmas blues *etc*
The Christmas tree is weeping
With candles all aglow
You never tried to kiss me
Beneath the mistletoe
Our revels now have ended
It's all gone awfully wrong
So join me in the singing
Of this bitter Christmas song

I've got the Christmas blues *etc*

Barry's Black Eyes

I've seen the beauty of Barry's black eyes
Eyes of a mystic who's not very wise
Angel of death from some lost paradise
I'm haunted by Barry's black eyes

I've heard the beating of Barry's black heart
After he's practised his turbulent art
Watching him sleep as the darkness departs
I ponder on Barry's black heart

I've heard the beating of Barry's black wings
Hidden my eyes from the mischief he brings
Suffered the outrageous arrows and slings
To fly upon Barry's black wings

Missed Understandings

Alas for our missed understandings
The way that we played hide and seek
Alas for our unhappy landings
The words that we never could speak

Perhaps I was much too demanding
And you not the straightest of men
Alas for our missed understandings
I wish we could do it again

I've learned how ambition can burn you
And battles can leave you with scars
I'd give all I've got to return to
Those missed understandings of ours

Come With Me

Come with me, go with me, burn with me, glow with me
Write me a sonnet or two
Sleep with me, wake with me, give with me, take with me
Love me the way I love you

Let me get high with you, laugh with you, cry with you
Be with you when I am blue
Rest with you, fight with you, day with you, night with you
Love me whatever I do

Work with me, play with me, run with me, stay with me
Make me your partner in crime
Handle me, fondle me, cradle me tenderly
Say I'm your reason and rhyme

Pray with me, sin with me, lose with me, win with me
Love me with all of my scars
Rise with me, fall with me, hide from it all with me
Nothing is mine now, it's ours

Depravity

Once you seemed much closer than my skin to me
We used to crawl inside your favourite symphony
And help each other hide out from reality
Now all we've got in common is depravity

I listened to your twisted brand of politics
Applauded when you did your famous parlour tricks
But now our long run fun affair is short of kicks
And all we've got in common is we need a fix

At first it was better than dreaming
Your hands and your lips made it real
I thought it was love we were making
But we were just making a deal

It's funny how we never seemed to separate
Since both of us are dreaming of another mate
Two melancholy monkeys in captivity
And all we've got in common is depravity

Semi-Detached

My sweetie and I are semi-detached
We're comfy and cool and perfectly matched
His lover is Ann. My lover is Art.
We're semi-detached but never apart

When some of our loves are semi-destroyed
We make it alright by quoting them Freud
We play little games and never get scratched
It's easy because we're semi-detached

Sometimes a playmate leaves us
For unconnected charms
But when a parting grieves us
We've got each other's arms

We each have a side that's free as the air
And people don't see the side that we share
Our set-up is sweet. There isn't a catch
The secret is living semi-detached

Dream Girl

I've got me a dream girl
Peaches and cream girl
The kind you see on the cover of
A shiny magazine

I met a pretty model
And took her home one night
I couldn't wait to kiss her
She seemed to be Miss Right
But she removed her lashes
And then her golden hair
And when she stood there ticking
She gave me quite a scare

But she was a dream girl *etc*

I took her and shook her
I wasn't being rude
But I was really bothered
When both her arms unscrewed
So then I grew suspicious
I tore off both her tits
And found that I was holding
Two lovely counterfeits

I was losing my dream girl *etc*

Beneath her chest of plastic
A nest of wires lurked
I studied her transistors
And saw the way she worked
I put her back together
She sure was full of life
And if you're ever out our way
Come by and meet the wife

The Game

The aim of the game
Is mainly in the pain
But it's so fascinating
The loving and the hating
The sighing and the praying
We've got to go on playing

The first few times it happened
We just couldn't work it out
But now we see the pattern
We know what it's all about

The aim of the game
Is mainly in the pain
A circle of frustration
Rejection and elation
Depression and obsession
A terrible connection

We're like compulsive gamblers
But our chips come from the heart
And we won't leave the table
Though the game tears us apart

The aim of the game
Is mainly in the pain
We're dizzy and despairing
But still we go on caring
Although the hurt keeps growing
Somehow it keeps us going
We've got to go on playing
The game

The Bitter Joys of Vinegar

The other day there came to me
A thought both sad and funny
You'll catch more flies with vinegar
Than you can catch with honey

I've given you my heart and shirt
Some laughs and poems and money
But you prefer her vinegar
You don't care much for honey

"You'll catch no flies with vinegar"
My mother used to say
But it's been my experience
It works the other way

I've seen her order you about
I've watched her crucify you
If I were made of sterner stuff
I'd torment and deny you

Instead of which I dote on you
And try to make life sunny
The bitter joys of vinegar
Entice you more than honey

Life Is a Bitch

Life is a bitch
From the cradle to the grave
Even when you're rich
You are always something's slave

Life is a bitch
Full of hang-ups, full of hurt
First love makes you itch
Then it dishes you the dirt

Just watch how the six-year-olds
Break each other's hearts
Better learn to stand the cold
Cultivate the arts

Life's full of shit
Even when you're in your prime
Though your show's a hit
Reason never seems to rhyme
Every joke has a switch
Every joker a twitch
Every high has a hitch
Baby, life is a bitch

Spring Can Really Hang You Up The Most

Spring this year has got me feeling
Like a horse that never left the post
I lie in my room staring up at the ceiling
Spring can really hang you up the most

College boys are writing sonnets
In the tender passion they're engrossed
But I'm on the shelf with last year's Easter bonnets
Spring can really hang you up the most

All afternoon those birds twitter-twit
I know the tune "This is love! This is it!"
Spring came along, season of song
Full of sweet promise but something went wrong

Doctors once prescribed a tonic
Sulphur and molasses was the dose
Didn't help a bit. My condition must be chronic
Spring can really hang you up the most

All alone the party's over
Old man Winter was a gracious host
But when you keep praying for snow to hide the clover
Spring can really hang you up the most

She Used To Sing
(Another Look At Mother)

Hard to believe that she used to sing
When she tucked you into bed
Hard to believe that she used to laugh
And her hair was henna red

Hard to believe she was ever young
That she tasted any joy
Hard to believe that her heart could melt
In the arms of any boy

Her life was not a hard one
She lived quite well
And why she's grown so bitter
Is more than I can tell

Hard to believe that you loved her so
For she's grown so mean and small
Seeing her now you just can't believe
That she ever sang at all

Mystery Man

I wish you'd tell me what you want and who you are
I wonder just what kind of life you're looking for
At times you seem so full of light, so bright and pure
I don't believe you're playing games but I'm not sure

You speak in accents of affection
But never give your heart away
Are people coins in your collection?
And will you spend them all some day?

I'm vain enough to think that I could find a cure
For maladies your mind has made, but I'm not sure
You tell me how the friends you have are using you
Perhaps you feel that way because you do it too

You seem to thrive on complications
I have to smile when you complain
Do you invent these situations?
Is it your stars that are to blame?

I've heard that there are one or two who you've betrayed
You say that other hands upset the plans you made
I'm half afraid that knowing you may leave a scar
I wonder if you know yourself just who you are

Boy

Naked boy in a green feather boa
Lit by gas fire
Did I dream you?

Smiling shy on the Indian pillows
Pale hair shining
Please remember

Did you come on some tornado
From the land of Oz
All decked out in emerald feathers
Stranded in this cloudy country?

Were you one of my inventions?
Whisper to me now
Did we ever melt together
By the pink light of the gas fire?

Naked boy in a green feather boa
Paint your eyelids
Let me dream you
One more time

The Prince Of Swords

Self-crowned protector of the wounded
Self-crowned destroyer of the strong
What am I doing in your movie?
How long, oh love, how long?

Many are ready to acclaim you
Many will follow where you lead
How can you keep your wine unwatered
With all those loves to feed

Once you appeared in armour shining
Once I was captured by your smile
Now I can see you as my killer
The jury at my trial

Do you remember winter landscapes
Nutcakes and figs and china tea?
Fire-lit your hands were warm and gentle
Your sword was sheathed in me

You try to train me like a falcon
I have my sky dream to protect
So you select another lover
Who shows you more respect

I could have stood your other lovers
I could have let you travel free
If you had found in all your bounty
One special place for me

I'll fly away before I'm broken
Leaving you satin and a song
Self-crowned protector of the wounded
Self-crowned destroyer of the strong

What Am I Doin' With You?

I'm always cold, you're always hot
I'm all worn out when you are not
I sit and watch, you want to dance
I play it safe, you take a chance
Oh baby, what am I doin' with you?

You like the woods, I like the town
You're mostly up, I'm mostly down
I sip champagne, you guzzle beer
But there's some reason why you're here
Oh baby, what am I doin' with you?

You want to go, I'd rather not
I'm always cold, you're always hot
But when you're hot and holding me
Somehow we manage to agree
Oh baby, what would I do without you?

Sadie-May Play

Master and slave, master and slave
Give us a taste of the lash that we crave
Everyone's playing from cradle to grave
We all misbehave

Pleasure and pain, pleasure and pain
Playing with fire, the whip and the chain
Is there a secret locked up in my brain?
Let's bring back the cane

Destruction used to be my aim
Now I'm sick of it
It takes two fools to play this game
And I want to quit

User and used, user and used
I play the victim, betrayed and abused
Let's stop the game, I'm no longer amused
And I don't want to play
Not today anyway

Do You Remember?

We've known each other ages and over oceans too
And in the times we never meet I often think of you
The last time that I saw you you were leaving for the coast
You came into my bed that night just like a gentle ghost

Do you remember?
You rubbed my back and stroked my hair
But in the morning
It seemed like you were never there

You left me in the kitchen and you muttered something dumb
And no one there would ever guess how close we almost come
The songs we made together had a flavour of their own
But they were always second to the songs you made alone

Do you remember?
You rubbed my back and stroked my hair
But in the morning
It seemed like you were never there
Seemed just like you were never there at all

The "If" Game

If you had been...if we had seen..or I knew when...
If we had gone three years ago instead of then

If I'd found the time
If you'd really tried
If I could have seen
What you always hide

If we had met...If he had come..If they had said...
That plane we missed...If you had found...If I had read...

If you hadn't run
If I'd been more free
You wouldn't be you
I wouldn't be me

Tennis, Anyone? (A Tango)

We're playing a game of tennis without a ball
In a garden where the flowers never fall
And after the game we'll go in to have our tea
The teacups are empty, so are your eyes on me

We're sitting beside a fire that's never lit
And you hold me but somehow we never fit
You put on a record throbbing with silent drums
And outside the window twilight will never come

I try so hard to reach you
My fingers press your face
But somehow in between us
Are miles and miles of empty space

I'm trying to find some reason for you to stay
But we both admit there's nothing left to say
Your footsteps still echo faintly along the hall
I glance in the mirror, no one is there at all

Burned

He was steely, he was salty
He was crazy, he was wise
There are two holes in the carpet
That he burned there with his eyes
Just staring at the carpet
He burned it with his eyes
With his eyes, with his eyes
With his holy madman's eyes

He was with me all one summer
On the California sands
There are two scars on my shoulders
Where he burned me with his hands
He touched my skin so gently
He burned me with his hands
With his hands, with his hands
With his holy con man's hands

He's an eloquent liar, he's a dreamer in red
He's a teacher on fire and a killer in bed
He keeps writing me letters from wherever he lands
And the pain gets no better but I can understand

He got restless in the autumn
And he drifted toward the south
There are marks upon the pillow
Where he burned it with his mouth
He left my mind on fire
He burned me with his mouth
With his mouth, with his mouth
With his holy poet's mouth
And his holy con man's hands
And his holy madman's eyes

Song Of The Procrastinating Penitent

When Dante saw the souls in hell
The burning and the frozen
His guide said, "Do not pity them,
Man, that's the scene they've chosen"
The flames of Hades used to wait
For anyone who fell
They must have been brave sinners then
When men believed in hell

Oh Lord I wanna be good
Dear Lord I wanna be good
Sweet Lord I wanna be good
But please not right away

Sometimes I dream there's still a chance
The Devil's gonna get me
I'd like to quit this awful life
But the music just won't let me
I try to keep my hands off you
I try to stay away
But I would gamble all my soul
To have you one more day

Oh Lord I wanna be good
Dear Lord I wanna be good
Good Lord I wanna be good
But please not right away
Sweet Lord I'm gonna be good
Tomorrow not today

The flames of Hades used to wait
For anyone who fell
They must have been brave sinners then
When men believed in hell

The Ballad Of The Sad Young Men

All the sad young men
Sitting in the bars
Knowing neon lights,
Missing all the stars

All the sad young men
Drifting through the town
Drinking up the night
Trying not to drown

Sing a song of sad young men
Glasses full of rye
All the news is bad again
Kiss your dreams goodbye

All the sad young men
Seek a certain smile
Someone they can hold
For a little while

Tired little girl
Does the best she can
Trying to be gay
For a sad young man

Autumn turns the leaves to gold
Slowly dies the heart
Sad young men are growing old
That's the cruellest part

While a grimy moon
Watches from above
All the sad young men
Play at making love

Misbegotten moon
Shine for sad young men
Let your gentle light
Guide them home again
All the sad young men

Personals

Here in a magazine
Buy it and read
All of the lonely ones
Crying their need
Boy wanted, girl wanted
Man seeking friend
Who ever answers them?
How does it end?

They put their loneliness
Into an ad
Isn't it laughable?
Isn't it sad?
Boy wanted, girl wanted
Longing to meet
Old-fashioned, up-to-date
Clean and discreet

Over-worked investment broker
Planning to relax
Seeking sexy, blonde deduction
From his income tax
Convent-bred, confused young lady
Looking for a guide
Gentleman with private income
Hasn't any pride

Easy to laugh at them
That's understood
You've been the lucky one
You've got it good
Boy wanted, girl wanted
Man seeking friend
Who ever answers them?
How does it end?

Why

Why is my every love a loss?
Why do our letters always cross?
Why do I always talk too much?
Why does it take so long to touch?

Why is my wisdom just a waste?
Why can't I rest alone and chaste?
Why won't I learn what time has taught?
Why am I always getting caught?

Why do I wear this foolish grin?
What would I do if I should win?
Should I be asking more or less?
Why is my every love a mess?

The Things We Never Did

When I think of all the things we never did together
The sunsets and the sights we never shared
I sigh a little sigh, but life speeds right on by
And mocks us for the time we never spared

I remember all the trips we never took together
The trains we missed, the hills we never climbed
I never understood why somehow we never could
And now you're walking ghostly in my mind

Everywhere I wander, everywhere I roam
All our long lost hours follow me back home

I regret the many talks we never had together
And I'm sorry for the secret selves we hid
Although we rarely meet, it's always bitter sweet
Just to dream of all the things we never did

The Early Winds of Morning

In the early winds of morning
She hurries home to bed
And a hundred happy pictures
Are dancing in her head

As she races with her shadow
Chased by the rising sun
She feels guilty and delighted
And proud of what she's done

The early winds of morning are singing to her lover
He can see her in the mirror as he shaves
And his hand's a little shaky as he lives the long night over
And he wonders if it's true that Jesus saves

As she tiptoes down the hallway
She cringes at each creak
And her heart is beating loudly
Her knees are feeling weak

She slips in beside her husband
That boring, snoring heap
And the early winds of morning
Will send her off to sleep

The Unruly Mistress

You come to me complaining about your mistress
You tell me she's become a nagging wife
The lady that you said
Was fabulous in bed
And brought such sauce and sunshine to your life

You say she's got the bad taste to criticise you
She makes demands, she cavils and complains
She isn't satisfied with polishing your pride
And keeping your self image free from stains

Well, I know all about you dear
Your boredom and your glory
And I must say I'd like to hear
Miss Pamela's side of the story

You come to me complaining about your mistress
Her lack of tact has cut you like a knife
While I stay safe at home
And write this little poem
And play the part of understanding wife

The Tigers Of Pain

The tigers of pain
Prowl out in the rain
Not far from the circle of light
Behind our locked doors
Their passionate roars
Assault us by day and by night

The famines and wars
On faraway shores
Send echoes that batter your heart
There's fire and flood
And spilling of blood
You wait for your troubles to start

When love comes along
Your head's full of song
It's hard to stay sober and sane
But be on your guard
For out in the yard
Are the terrible tigers of pain

Why Should Love Be So Hard On The Heart

Why should love be so hard on the heart
Why does it caress you then tear you apart
Why does it fool you, why does it tease you
Why does it scare you, why does it please you

Why should love be so loaded with pain
Why does it betray you again and again
Why does the promise fade so unfairly
Why does the magic happen so rarely

Ah, those wonderful wild men
They hammer your heart like a fist
You spend your time yearning and sighing and burning
While they're always out getting pissed

Why should love be so tied up in knots
Well either it's that or it's making cheap shots
It gives us a kick and inspires our art
But why should love be so hard on the heart

Times are changing they tell us
There must be a new way to live
Alongside a new love, a tender and true love
Who'll gladly return what we give

Why should love be so much on the mind
It staggers our senses and makes us all blind
There must be an answer, we're all so damn smart
So why should love be so hard on the heart

Cri de Cœur
(from the French of Jacques Prévert)

It's not just my voice that is singing
There are voices from the past
There is the sound of church-bells ringing
And some dreams that didn't last
There are the desperate and the gay
The siren song of yesterday
The voice of all my youthful follies
And the one that got away

There is the voice of Sister Sorrow
And the voice of fleeting joy
There is the voice of some tomorrow
That this moment may destroy
There is a fugitive who drowns
A little girl in Mother's gowns
The voice of one more fallen sparrow
That's been broken by this town

And always, always when I'm singing
That bird sings along with me
Although in pain its notes are ringing
In the face of destiny
If I could tell you all it sings
About the winters and the springs
When I was hungry and tormented
By misfortune's wicked stings

But I'd do better to forget it
For that song's no longer mine
I'm going on to something sweeter
Than that shabby Auld Lang Syne
Don't want to suffer any more
I'm gonna get up off the floor
Although my dearest friend Miss Fortune
Says 'I've heard that song before'

I'm going to wipe away my teardrops
I won't advertise my pain
'Cause all my two-a-penny troubles
Aren't enough to stop the train
Right now I'm on my way to Spain
Through all the sunsets and the rain
And if this planet doesn't suit me
I'm not coming here again

And if the living dead officials
At the customs stop me there
Just let them vandalise my baggage
I've got nothing to declare
Love may be on another train
But we are sure to meet again
For just like me love is a wanderer
And we're sure to meet again

So Says My Song

Why can't I write a happy song
With bluebirds singing all day long
Why do the storm clouds hide the sun
In all my songs

Why can't I sing of honey days
A song of joy, a song of praise
Why must I sing of all the ways
That love goes wrong

I may write a verse that is funny
But mostly laments are my thing
For somehow the song of the honey
Seems less than the song of the sting

Why can't I chant the positive
Because I find it hard to live
With all the hurts that love can give
So says my song

And earth is fair and flesh is fine
There's wine to share for Auld Lang Syne
But death is still the bottom line
So says my song

It Isn't Such A Bad Life After All

After all the sunshine and the rain
After all the pleasure and the pain
Seems to me I really can't complain
And it isn't such a bad life after all

After all the star-dust and the rainbows
After all the suppers and the songs
After all the lovely music makers
It seems to me that nothing's really wrong
And it isn't such a bad life after all

Why was I so frightened
To have you by my side
Convinced that love was tragic
Can it be that all those poets lied?

After all the uppers and downers
Cloudy days when I was sore distressed
After all the laughter and the lovers
It seems to me that I've been truly blessed

No it's not a sad life
When all is said and done
The load keeps getting lighter
And I'll admit I've had a lot of fun

After all the weekends in the country
Knowing kids and flowers face to face
After all these travels I've decided
This planet is a fine and pleasant place
It seems to me I've reached a state of grace
And it isn't such a bad life after all

Love's Eyes

Love comes along with sweet death in her eyes
Leading you down to a tunnel of sighs
Whispering secrets and old alibis
With death in her eyes

Love comes along with a knife in her hands
Armed with the secret of life in her hands
Swinging her hips to the beat of the bands
A knife in her hands

Love comes along like some God in disguise
Opening doors to a dark paradise
Scary, seductive, the ultimate prize
With life in her hands
And death in her eyes

chorus: Singing honey come here
           Tonight is the night
           Then she blows in your ear
           And out goes the light